THE GREAT FRAUD

UPON

THE PUBLIC CREDULITY

IN THE

ORGANIZATION OF THE REPUBLICAN PARTY

UPON

THE RUINS OF THE "WHIG PARTY,"

AN ADDRESS TO THE OLD-LINE WHIGS OF THE UNION.

WASHINGTON:
PRINTED AT THE UNION OFFICE.
1856.

THE DUTY OF THE WHIGS TO THE AMERICAN UNION.

Human society could not long exist without government; the strong would crush out the weak, the ignorant would fall victims to the wise, and the whole would be destroyed by the conflict of its parts.

In the present condition of human nature, laws, and their corresponding appendages, are not only a blessing, for which man should be thankful, but a necessity, without which he could not live at all.

It is not a good argument against the propriety of law, and in favor of anarchy, that, under every form of government, and in the complicated working of every system of laws, injustice may be done to a larger or smaller portion of the community. This has always been the case, and most likely always will be, until angels instead of men dispense the laws.

There can be no condition of society so perfect, or the administration of its laws so impartial, but that some classes of the people will have apparent grounds of complaint against the unequal burdens which seem to rest upon them. This complaint will always be directed against the ruling power as the nearest *perceivable* cause, whilst the *real* cause, however, is not necessarily in the government, but results from the frail and corrupted condition of the nature of man himself, both the governors and the governed, and is quite as visible in all of the other relations of life as in the civil government.

The republican has this eminent superiority over every other form of government—that if the people are badly governed, unjustly dealt with, or severely oppressed, they feel that it has been the result of their own choice, and that the evil to be corrected is within their own power. The form of government under which we live has much to do with the laws which are made to sustain it, with the administration which executes it, and the happiness, peace, and prosperity which the people enjoy under it. But the security of the citizen under any form of government is dependent entirely upon the supremacy of clearly defined, well understood, and unquestionably just laws, impartially administered in the spirit of charity.

In regard to civil government, as to all other subjects, differences of opinion must exist upon all questions where the truth is not clearly self-evident, of which character there are but few truths. This difference of opinion must induce a corresponding difference of action. Upon questions of policy or government, it of necessity arrays men into parties. In monarchical governments this difference of opinion finds its way to the public mind through literary journals, romances, stage and plays, among the more intelligent, and in songs and proverbs among the laboring classes. In republics, where the government emanates from the free expression of the will, and the voluntary action of the people, party is its natural offspring. Such parties have always existed; such parties we now have; and to their mutual vigilance we will always be indebted for the efficiency and purity of our present political system. If we would have these parties efficient, they must be preserved in purity; and they can be kept pure only by an unflinching adherence to well-settled principles.

A real statesman never can be governed by mere party. Party may very properly be used as the machinery by which principles do their work. Openly conducted, and justly administered, party organizations are essential to the safety and purity of our government itself, if party be made subservient to principle. But where *principles* are made subservient to party considerations or party success, civil government has no guaranty for either its protection or its perpetuity. The true doctrine of *pure* republicanism is this: make party your servant; to be corrected when wrong; to be cherished when right; to be abandoned when it becomes either corrupt or incorrigible. Let principle be your master—your supreme ruler. Parties are the creatures of circumstances. They grow up hastily—are short lived; they serve the purposes of government, or become the engines of corruption. They then die out, and leave not so much as a shadow or a ghost behind them to fill up their place, or mark the remembrance of their being.

Principles live forever. Justice, truth, and purity are co-eval and co-eternal with God himself; in every climate, under every form of government, among all nations of the earth, these great principles have been cardinal. For the time being, they may have been shrouded in darkness, embarrassed by the interference of unwise government, but they have never been crushed out. They have always found some place, though obscure it may have been, to vindicate their supremacy and assert their eternity. Good men, in power, have been governed by these principles; bad men, in suffering, have appealed to them, not in vain, for protection and redress. All men give assent to them, though they may disregard their restrictions or neglect their injunctions.

Political parties have no right to plead exemption from the moral obligations of these principles—this is always true; but it comes with greater force at a time when all parties are dissolving; when old and well-established and great truths are abandoned; when factions and cliques and secret lodges are banding together for purposes of political power, and personal emolument, defiant of national happiness, and reckless of the national existence. Just such times are now upon the country. Old party lines have been obliterated; entirely new party organizations are being formed all over the country, based upon entirely new political doctrines, and inviting the people to issues no less perilous than extraordinary. One section of the Union is arrayed against the other; one great branch of the Christian church is making political war upon the other; local interests and local prejudices are put in conflict with national law and the administration of the general government. Never since the Declaration of our Independence has the public mind been so unsettled, and the peace of the country so imperilled as it now is.

As citizens of a common country, and believers in a common Christian faith, it is a duty we owe to the great cause of civilization over the whole earth, which is dependent to a great extent upon the success of our government, and the stability of our institutions; a duty we owe to our posterity who will prosper for ages under our liberal institutions transmitted to them, or perish in the general wreck of this free government; a duty we owe to God, who hath made the prosperity of all government dependent upon the strict justice of its rulers, and the quiet submission of the people to the laws of the country, to carefully take our steps in the determination of our destiny as a government, and our happiness as a people.

In such confusion as now surrounds us, we can mark out for ourselves no safe pathway of duty, until we carefully examine the starting-point of our political faith, and carefully consider what *we ought to be*, and as calmly reflect upon *what we are.*

In the year 1852, we were at peace with the whole world; our ships were laden with the riches of the land, and carried food and raiment to every portion of the habitable globe; our fields were rich with the fruits of a bounteous harvest; our people were employed, and the whole country presented a prosperity and happiness without a precedent or parallel in our history; benevolent societies were forming in every part of the country for the relief of distress and the amelioration of the wants and sufferings of the benighted people of foreign lands; our churches were crowded with penitent sinners and devoted Christians, and a general revival of religion was spreading throughout the nation; agricultural fairs were forming for the development of the resources of our wealth; railroad companies were organizing for the facilitation of our internal commerce; gold commenced to be poured in from California; myriads of population were emigrating to the western States; the wages of labor were highly remunerative, and our people were profitably employed and contented. So little did the country feel concerned for our political welfare, and so confident were the people of our continued peace, that both political parties adopted substantially a common platform.

The Whig platform of 1852 is undoubtedly the most candid, clear, and unquestionable exposition of the sentiments, and feelings, and doctrines of that party which has ever been given to the country.

THE WHIG PLATFORM OF 1852.

"The Whigs of the United States, in convention assembled, firmly adhering to the great conservative republican principle by which they are controlled and governed, and now, as ever, relying upon the intelligence of the American people, with an abiding confidence in their capacity for self-government, and their continued devotion to the Constitution and the Union, do proclaim the following as the political sentiments and determination, fo the establishment and maintenance of which their national organization, as a party, is effected:

"1. That the government of the United States is of a limited character, and it is confined to the exercise of powers expressly granted by the Constitution, and such as may be necessary and proper for carrying the granted powers into full execution; and that all powers not thus granted or necessarily implied are expressly reserved to the States respectively, and to the people.

"2 That the State governments should be held secure in their reserved rights, and the general government sustained in its constitutional powers, and the Union should be revered and watched over as the palladium of our liberties.

"3. That, while struggling freedom everywhere enlists the warmest sympathy of the Whig party, we still adhere to the doctrines of the Father of his Country, as announced in his Farewell Address of keeping ourselves free from all entangling alliances with foreign countries, and of never quitting our own to stand upon foreign ground; that our mission as a Republic is not to propagate our opinions, or impose on other countries our form of government by artifice or force, but to teach by example, and show by our success, moderation, and justice, the blessings of self-government, and the advantages of free institutions.

"4. That where the people make and control the government they should obey its Constitution, laws, and treaties, as they would retain their self-respect, and the respect which they claim and will enforce from foreign powers.

"5. That the government should be conducted upon principles of the strictest economy, and that revenue sufficient for the expenses of its economical administration in time of peace ought to be mainly derived from a duty on imports, and not from direct taxes; and, in levying such duties, sound policy requires a just discrimination, whereby suitable encouragement may be afforded to American industry, equally to classes, and to all portions of the country

"6 That the Constitution vests in Congress the power to open and repair harbors, and remove obstructions from navigable rivers; and it is expedient that Congress should exercise that power whenever such improvements are necessary for the common defence, or for the protection and facility of commerce with foreign nations or among the States—such improvements in every instance being national and general in their character.

"7. That the Federal and State governments are parts of one system, alike necessary for the common prosperity peace, and security, and ought to be regarded alike with a cordial, habitual, and immovable attachment. Respect for the authority of each, and the acquiescence in just constitutional measures of each, are duties required by the plainest considerations of national, of State, and of individual welfare.

"8. That the series of acts of the thirty-first Congress, the act known as the fugitive slave law included, are received and acquiesced in by the Whig party of the United States as a settlement, in principle and substance, of the dangerous and exciting questions which they embrace, and, so far as they are concerned, we will maintain them, and insist upon their enforcement until time and experience shall demonstrate the necessity of further legislation to guard against the evasion of the laws on the one hand, and the abuse of their powers on the other, not impairing their present efficiency; and we deprecate all further agitation of the questions thus settled as dangerous to our peace, and will discountenance all efforts to continue or renew such agitation, whenever, wherever, or however, the attempt may be made; and we will maintain this system as essential to the nationality of the Whig party, and the integrity of the Union."

The preamble declares the "abiding confidence" of the Whig party "in the capacity of the people to govern themselves."

The first resolution asserts the limited character of the powers of "the government of the United States."

The second resolution grows legitimately out of the first, and affirms "the doctrines of State sovereignty."

The third resolution is an expression of sympathy with the oppressed everywhere, upon the one hand, and, upon the other hand, an unyielding determination to adhere to the policy of Washington—to interfere with none of the revolutions, nor participate in the civil wars of other nations.

The fourth resolution is a pledge to the supremacy of the constitution and law in our own land, and the observance, in good faith, of treaties made with foreign powers.

The fifth resolution recommends a revenue tariff, which will give protection equally to the industry of every section of the Union.

The sixth resolution is an elimination of Congressional power, in the construction of internal improvements, to the specified grants of the constitution itself.

The seventh resolution is an affirmation of that State comity which, if exercised, will perpetuate us as one people for ages to come; but without which we can have no lasting existence as a confederated republic, and remain what we now are—*E Pluribus Unum*, to the glory of civil liberty, and the terror of tyrants.

The eighth resolution is a covenant to leave undisturbed the question of slavery and the social law of the country, allowing each section to form its own judgment, to pursue its own course, and determine its own action in relation to its own police laws and its own domestic institutions.

The foregoing resolutions are presented in detail and noted to prove that there is not one single element of the Republican party deducible or inferrible from, or in anywise affiliated with, the doctrines of the old Whig party.

DEMOCRATIC PLATFORM.

"*Resolved*, That the American democracy place their trust in the intelligence, the patriotism and the discriminating justice of the American people.

"*Resolved*, That we regard this as a distinctive feature of our creed, which we are proud to maintain before the world as a great element in a form of government springing from and upheld by a popular will; and we contrast it with the creed and practice of federalism, under whatever name or form, which seeks to palsy the vote of the constituent, and which conceives no imposture too monstrous for the popular credulity.

"*Resolved, therefore*, That, entertaining these views, the Democratic party of the Union, through their delegates, assembled in a general convention of the States, convening together in a spirit of concord, of devotion to the doctrines and faith of a free representative government, and appealing to their fellow-citizens for the rectitude of their intentions, renew and re-assert before the American people the declaration of principles avowed by them, when on former occasions, in general convention, they presented their candidates for the popular suffrages.

"1. That the federal government is one of limited powers, derived solely from the constitution, and the grants of power made therein ought to be strictly construed by all the departments and agents of the government; and that it is inexpedient and dangerous to exercise doubtful constitutional powers.

"2. That the constitution does not confer upon the general government the power to commence and carry on a general system of internal improvements.

"3. That the constitution does not confer authority upon the federal government, directly or indirectly, to assume the debts of the several States, contracted for local internal improvements, or other State purposes; nor would such assumption be just or expedient.

"4. That justice and sound policy forbid the federal government to foster one branch of industry to the detriment of any other, or to cherish the interests of one portion to the injury of another portion of our common country; that every citizen and every section of the country has a right to demand and insist upon an equality of rights and privileges, and a complete and ample protection of persons and property from domestic violence and foreign aggression.

"5. That it is the duty of every branch of the government to enforce and practise the most rigid economy in conducting our public affairs, and that no more revenue ought to be raised than is required to defray the necessary expenses of the government, and for the gradual but certain extinction of the public debt.

"6. That Congress has no power to charter a national bank; that we believe such an institution one of deadly hostility to the best interest of our country, dangerous to our republican institutions and the liberties of the people, and calculated to place the business of the country within the control of a concentrated money power, and above the laws and will of the people; and that the results of democratic legislation, in this and all other financial measures upon which issues have been made between the two political parties of the country, have demonstrated to practical men of all parties their soundness, safety, and utility in all business pursuits.

"7. That the separation of the moneys of the government from all banking institutions is indispensable for the safety of the funds of the government, and the rights of the people.

"8. That the liberal principles embodied by Jefferson in the Declaration of Independence, and sanctioned in the constitution, which makes ours the land of liberty and the asylum of the oppressed of every nation, have ever been cardinal principles of the democratic faith; and every attempt to abridge the privilege of becoming citizens and owners of soil amongst us ought to be resisted with the same spirit which swept the alien and sedition laws from our statute-book.

"9. That Congress has no power under the constitution to interfere with or control the domestic institutions of the several States, and that all such States are the sole and proper judges of everything appertaining to their own affairs not prohibited by the constitution; that all efforts of the Abolitionists, or others, made to induce Congress to interfere with questions of slavery, or to take incipient steps in relation thereto, are calculated to lead to the most alarming and dangerous consequences; and that all such efforts have an inevitable tendency to diminish the happiness of the people, and endanger the stability and permanency of the Union, and ought not to be countenanced by any friend of our political institutions."

This was the Democratic platform in the year 1852, differing in no cardinal principle or essential point from the one adopted by the Whig party. On these platforms the contest went to the people; to this point was the political controversy of the country narrowed down, and upon these issues did the contest end. After an honorable conflict of twenty years, the Democratic party gained a final victory.

Though defeated by an overwhelming majority, the Whig party magnanimously acquiesced in the election of President Pierce, and, by unanimous consent, agreed to present no factious opposition to his administration.

This election settled all the great questions of disputed national policy, and these two platforms formed the basis of the prospective course of both political parties.

In the mean time, a new and entirely different political organization had been quietly commenced, and incidentally alluded to by the editor of the New York Tribune. For the last twenty years, the political principles of this new organization, in another form and by another name, were thoroughly discussed, first in the New Yorker, afterwards in the Tribune, and finally by all of its satellites in every part of the northern States.

Up to the year 1852, for the purposes of preserving his political influence, and obtaining numerical strength in a final rupture of the Whig party which he anticipated, Hon. Horace Greeley announced through the Tribune that he would support the nominees of the Whig party, but would spit upon the platform, notwithstanding the principles of which the Whig candidates for President and Vice President had sacredly bound themselves to maintain. In other words, he volunteered his frieneship to ruin the party. No sooner had he accomplished his object, than he publicly announced the *death* of the Whig party.

Until now, the proper time had never presented itself for the practical adoption of his long-cherished social principles. He commenced the inauguration of his new party, by proposing moral questions for legislative action, which it had been the constitutional policy and determined purpose of our government forever to exclude from the arena of legislation.

In the early settlement of this country, our ancestors brought with them the established religion of their native land to their respective colonies. Religious institutions were supported by a direct tax, and ultimately, in some of the colonies, the right of opinion, the freedom of speech, and the liberty of conscience were entirely compromitted. This was arlarmingly true of some of the New England provinces.

In the formation of the constitution of the United States, our fathers put all questions of religious duty upon their true basis—upon man's direct personal responsibility to God; whilst the government offered perfect security to the life, liberty, property, and the pursuit of happiness of the citizen. It very properly committed the reformation of the world, and the cultivation of the graces of the heart, to the voluntary action of the people, under the moral teachings of Christ and his Apostles.

Those early proscriptions had thrown a gloom over the self-denying character, and otherwise chivalric and brilliant history of our ancestors. The framers of the constitution sought to prevent their recurrence by a special provision, that there should be no religious test required either as a condition of citizenship, or qualification for office. These great religious questions have never been introduced anywhere into the councils of civil government, without inducing civil war. They have uniformly sapped the foundations of civil liberty wherever they have been raised. But just such questions as these were proposed one by one for legislative action; they were intended ultimately to form the basis of a great party.

In different States of the Union, these questions were urged by the press which was under the control of the Tribune. The editor of the Tribune was in early life an avowed socialist, a follower of Fourrier. He talked, and wrote, and dreamed of an earthly millennium, which should be consummated by the advent of social reform. For years he made his press the lever-power of that system of reform. He pictured a beau ideal government, and inculcated notions of FRENCH LIBERTY and revolution of which this country is having just now quite enough. Others claim the paternity of this NEW SOCIAL PARTY, for such it is. But the editor of the New York Tribune is the father of the whole movement; for years it has been the nursling of his paper. Its varied forms, insinuating power, and prospective success, are entirely dependent upon his superior tact and thorough control of the public passion and intimate acquaintance with human character. If this party succeeds, its success will be monumental of the immortality of Horace Greeley; if it fails, Horace Greeley will live in history as its bold and ingenious architect, whilst all its elements, with its minor workers, will be buried in the rubbish of its ruins.

The initiatory step in this organization was an appeal to the moral sentiment of the country to correct its immoralities by positive legislation. The first great principle of morality brought before the public for its political action was—

THE CAUSE OF TEMPERANCE.

For more than a quarter of a century the people of the United States have been using every legitimate moral means for the reformation of intemperate men, who drank up their private fortunes, diseased their physical system, and ruined their families. To more effectually accomplish their purpose, they formed benevolent societies for the reformation of the drunkard, and the relief of his family. This good work extended over the whole country, and became a strong feature of the moral sentiment of the land. Nearly every public man became a member of the temperance society—the work was universally approved. The pulpit sent forth its plea; the minister of Christ wept over the victims of drunkenness, and appealed to them by prayers, and tears, and exhortations. Masonic lodges, Odd-Fellows' encampments, and rural neighborhoods were converted into temperance societies, and brought every conceivable influence to bear upon the drunkard and cure his infirmity. The moral standard of the country was elevated until it became a reproach to drink, or to be found in drinking-houses. The jubilee of sobriety was dawning upon the country, and the moral power of the Christian faith was becoming omnipotent. Such was the state of the country, and such the condition of the public mind, before the inauguration of this new party. Its leaders knew how strong a hold temperance had upon the popular feeling of the purest classes of society, and determined to direct that feeling as so much capital for their own political purposes. They proposed the thorough organization of the temperance forces in every neighborhood all over the whole country, with passwords, and grips, and countersigns, and songs, and festivals, and other extraordinary demonstrations. Upon the part of the people this was all done in good faith to arrest the evil of drunkenness. Upon the part of the politicians it was intended as but initiatory to ulterior and entirely different purposes. It was not long after these organizations were first instituted, that superannuated politicians, who had followed the fortunes of every political party, were found directing them. The "SONS OF TEMPERANCE," "GOOD TEMPLARS," "RECHABITES," and "GOOD SAMARITANS," were all lead by some zealous ex-member of the legislature, or other political aspirant, who, with wonderful self-denial, had abandoned their old political associations, and, with extraordinary devotion to their new moral faith, spent night and day in the organization of the various temperance orders. Temperance was now to assume a new position under the lead of these converted politicians. They cared not so much for the reformation of drunkards, as for the destruction of all dram-shops and still-houses. They discarded every manner of moral suasion as entirely inefficient. There was with them no cure for drunkenness, no hope for the drunkard but in legal suasion; not that legal suasion which punished drunkenness, and abolished drunken resorts. They counselled a temperance legislation which transcended all bounds of the ordinary law-making power in a free government. The law of nearly every State in the Union punished drunkenness and its consequent crimes. But they insisted upon the destruction of all liquors, and the absolute prohibition of all liquor-making, upon the same principle that you would cut out every man's tongue to prevent slander, or cut off every man's hand to prevent murder or theft.

In this wild excitement the sacred cause of Christianity and temperance, its purest virtue, were illegitimately dragged into the political arena. The true friends of sobriety were nobly working for this great reform in good faith, whilst these political reformers were turning the various temperance orders into political caucuses, in which they nominated candidates for civil office, and plans were laid for the control of elections. In thus making these orders the adjuncts of a political party, hundreds were seduced from their old party affinities, and abandoned entirely their party connexions.

Temperance reform was the ostensible object of this movement. The real object was the acquisition of political power, by assuming control over the popular feeling.

Strict and searching laws against drunkenness have stood upon the statute-book of every State in the Union, and Congress has made severe police laws against drunkenness, and where it has been found necessary for the preservation of the peace of society, has made the liquor traffic highly penal. In some of the States grog-shops were declared a nuisance, and indictable as such, by positive law. It was generally conceded that everything which law could profitably do had been already done. But with the reformers there were two inseparable objections to the existing laws. The first objection was this: that those laws had been made under the direction and auspices of the old parties, and of course could create no political capital for this new organization. The second objection was a cardinal one of great force.

Under the existing law there was no patronage to dispense; whilst, under the contemplated legislation, there were to be county agencies, search warrants, and neighborhood spies. Liquor-selling would now be legal, and honorably conducted under the auspices of *total abstinence.* Constables, young village lawyers, would find abundant employ in enforcing temperance laws and quelling mobs. It was well known that this would invite resistance to the law itself upon the part of the liquor dealers. Then would follow the destruction of their property, and the arrest of the offenders. It was well calculated that all these feuds and broils would generate a perpetual excitement, and secure the aid of the moral force of the country in building up a party for entirely irrelevant political purposes. This was the basis of their action upon the temperance question, and such were the means brought to bear to make it a powerful auxiliary of this political party. They inflamed the fanaticism of the people until their legislative demands knew no bounds. Even before the passage of the law could be effected, mobs were raised to tear down houses and pour out liquors, to frustrate the real objects of the temperance movement, and make it subservient to their ambitions. In the passage of the law an inquisitorial system was adopted which contravened all the well-established principles of the right of property and private judgment. They assumed supreme authority over the appetites and the business of private men.

Like every other unconstitutional assumption of legislative power, these laws have produced a fearful reaction of the public mind, and such is now the state of indignation against this untimely and mercenary interference, that it will require the most watchful and prudent supervision and direction of the true temperance men, to preserve the temperance cause itself from contempt.

No sooner had this political conquest been made over the virtues of the people by heartless demagogues, than THEY were found perpetrating an insult upon the injured enterprise of the temperance reformation.

To make their perfidy complete, these very same men are celebrating, with wines and brandy and punch, railroad conventions, New-Year festivities, political parties, and private social gatherings.

It was a great wrong perpetrated upon the public passion to drive it to madness, and make a great Christian virtue the pretext for invading the private rights and family sanctuary with impudent spies and pragmatical officials.

In our sober moments it alarms us that it was ever dreamed of as right to send constables into the sideboard and bureau, the bed-chamber and closet of a quiet Christian family, to know what they ate and what they drank.

But that was not the only or the most fearful wrong which was done to the country: that wrong was remediable; the people had the redress in thair own hands; they had no difficulty in determining and falling back upon their own legitimate rights. But morality was stabbed to the heart under a false name, and her life-blood is dripping down at her feet. *Real* temperance men, who regard temperance in its true light as the very highest and purest element of Christian character, now feel that the cause has been struck down in the prostituted name of friendship. The ordinary temperance appeals, though made in good faith by good men, are assailed by suspicion and confounded with politics; nor, until the last lingering element of political chicanery has been separated from the cause of temperance, can the lovers of sobriety hope again to enter the field in successful contest against the wide-spreading vice of drunkenness. The land is filled with drunkenness; our strong men are swept away by its fires like leaves in a burning forest. But so effectually have these political temperance men hedged up our pathway, that we dare not now call up the subject in sermons or speeches without becoming obnoxious to the charge of an illegitimate interference, under the cover of morality, with the politics of the country.

Temperance men committed a folly when they did not repulse these political intruders when they first put their unholy feet upon the threshold of the temperance movement. In the coming campaign the Republican party will obey the mandates and follow the course indicated by the New York Tribune, their leader. Where the temperance question may be made available, it will be the movement, paramount to all others. Where it would hang as a weight upon the success of the Republican party, it will be thrown aside as an entirely secondary matter, having no connexion whatever with politics. Such has been their tactics, and such are the abuses that have been of the temperance question by this party. What is now the condition of temperance in the country; of societies laboring for the reformation of the inebriate, blessed and loved by everybody? We have county groceries, and liquor agencies, kept by political partisans, who are appointed by the dominant political party according to his political complexion, without any other regard whatever; and the whole now amounts to nothing more nor less than the monopoly of the whiskey business to reward partisans; for it is notorious that whiskey is everywhere given out to all who seek it, with or without a just pretence under the law. After the temperance question had been taxed to its utmost capacity for the benefit of the party, the editor of the New York Tribune came out in a long article, coolly informing the country that, though he had always been an ardent temperance man, he attached no importance to the question of temperance when compared with the great question now at issue before the country—the triumph of the Republican party.

FOURRIERISM.—THE EMANCIPATION AND EQUALITY OF THE BLACKS.

The next element which entered into the organization of this party, had its diversified beginnings under the auspices of Garrison, Gerrit Smith, Joshua R. Giddings, Thompson, of England, and other misguided philanthropists, who looked to the ultimate emancipation of the slaves, and the political and social equality of all the races; the common distribution and enjoyment of the offices, honors, and wealth of society among all men. They painted their republic upon canvass, and presented in a captivating style, upon paper, their purely imaginary society; a condition of society such as has never existed anywhere; a state of things which has never been promised in the most thorough reformation of human nature in this world; such as was denied to our patriarchal fathers, which was beyond the asserted control of the Saviour himself in his mission among men, and which is in direct contravention of the unfulfilled prophecies of Christ and his Apostles for all time to come. But such was their hope. Its futility will be examined.

There is an unspeakable difference between the highest conceivable good as it exists in the imagination of the Utopian, and that other practical real good as it has descended to us in the history of human governments, and as it develops itself in the existing elements of human society. Let us see what is that difference between what is real and what is imaginary. I have been taught that the ultimate reward of the *Christian* in his HOME of Heaven shall be *perfect*. I can conceive a condition of man immortalized, where every sense shall be perfect, and every perception will be accurate—where the eye, freed from disease, shall give to the soul a vision of truth, and beauty, and comprehension, that could correctly, with ineffable pleasure, and at a single glance, grasp the architecture and solve the mysteries of the firmament—sensitive to all symmetry and impervious to all pain. I can conceive how the ear, strung to "the concord of sweet sounds," may extract from the voice of the elements all their harmony, and be deaf to all their discord; the thunders of the last judgment and the convulsions of a dying universe would be sweet, like the music of the voice of many waters. I can conceive how all the senses may be avenues of unmixed pleasure, with health and perfection to guard them against the invasions of pain or decay. Nor do my imagnations cease here. I can conceive how the intellectual powers of man may be elevated above error and passion, and impurity. I can conceive how the reason of a perfect mind may be exalted above fallacy or imposition; how the memory might cling to every transpiring event, and treasure it up as its own; how imagination, assisted by memory, could foresee with certainty truths now shrouded in the distance of time. I can conceive how the unclad soul, relieved of the slavish mantle of flesh, would forever aspire after and assimilate itself to the pure character of God. Nor has it been placed beyond the reach of human conception, for it has been addressed to human belief, how the body itself may be made incorruptible and immortal, and, like asbestos in the furnace, burn in eternal beauty. I can portray to my mind a condition of society where all are equals and friends, bound together in chains of harmony and love as a great family, only subject to the supreme power of the Great Ruler of all things, elevated far above suffering and sustained without sympathy, fed by the hand of the Almighty. This is what I can imagine, and the joys of Heaven are "*more*" than man can "*conceive*." But it is not beneath the dignity of the philosopher to come down from the regions of fancy and carefully examine the real condition of society as it now is—as it always must be—in this world. The real difficulty in the solution of man's earthly wrongs and sufferings is clearly and correctly presented by Israel's mightiest king in Holy Writ—"*The heart of man is deceitful above all things and desperately wicked.*"

Let us look at man in the different stages of life and death, just as he is, and see how it compares or contrasts with the condition of our beau ideal man in our visionary society. Let us mark his moral condition. In the hour of death—this is the most sacred time in man's earthly being—the circumstances that surround him, the deeds of his life that pursue him, the terrible judgment and consequent responsibility that lift themselves up before him, combine to indicate to his own mind the terrible necessity of personal purity, and mental and moral perfection. He feels this as he never felt it before. But even here, where, at the bidding of God, angels keep watch over the destiny of the dying, long-treasured malice and revenge still linger around the very holy of the holies of the heart. Insatiate ambition grasps with its faltering arm at every fleeting object of power that dances before its beclouded vision; even envy is not satisfied with the gnawings of a life-time, but sits fault-finding at the portals of the grave.

But you may look after man still further: take the very highest order of man, A CHRISTIAN, in the very *holiest* place where man holds converse with God—at the sacramental board; here he swears allegiance to his Saviour by the blood which warmed his Saviour's heart, which sits in symbols before him; here he is in full view of the commanding majesty of Heaven, with the excruciating torture of the cross; the unaffected simplicity of the life and the spotless innocence of the character of the Saviour, the disinterested benevolence of the immortal God, graphically pictured to his mind, and compassionately appealing to his heart—here, where the footsteps of angels are carefully taken, the wild passions of man's wicked nature leap over all these hallowed environments; here avarice looks with undaunted impudence in the very face of benevolence; impurity and crime claim for themselves a lurking-place in the heart of the Christian, and the devil disputes for dominion in the temple of God.

Follow man further still: go with him into the congregation of religious worshippers, where on the Sabbath day good men meet to rest from the labors of the week; here, where the world is shut out, still the world comes in; follow him out into society as it exists in our own country, where the prime object of law is to secure equality and freedom to the citizen; what do you see? Do not the rich grind the face of the poor? Do not the learned take advantage of the ignorant? Do not the strong bear down the weak? And, in the precious name of liberty, are not whole communities openly defrauded of their dearest rights?

What is the condition of society in the great city of New York—the metropolis of the western world? Here restrictive laws have brought all their powers to bear upon the evils of society for their correction. Here a standing army of police officers claim supervision, under positive law, over the dwellings, and business, and intercourse of the people. Does society here present the reflex of our Utopian government—our imaginary human happiness and human perfection?

Is it not true that in the evening shadow of the Tribune office there is now reigning among the lower classes of the people a superstition, (consisting of spiritual rappings, table-turnings, fortune-telling, necromancy, clairvoyance, &c.,) as gloomy as the powowings of heathen worship in the darkest ages of the world? Is there not in New York city, now, a barbarism comprising prize-fights, street mobs, midnight orgies, highway robberies, and petty pilferings, revolting to civilization, as terrible as the savage rule of the Camanches? Is there not a feverish and loathsome licentiousness as vile as the abominations of the Sandwich Islands? Of the one million of inhabitants who live in this vast metropolis, is there one prudent man of property who ventures to lie down at night without locking his door to secure his house from the invasion of burglars? or who feels a surprise to hear, when he rises in the morning, that innocent strangers have been murdered in the streets in the silent hours of midnight?

All conditions of human society, from the highest to the lowest, must feel the necessary inquietude of the governed—the impracticability of a just and impartial administration of government, so as to prevent complaint, and the constant dangers to which every member of society is exposed, whether with or without government.

The source of much of the disquiet of the people at existing laws is a misapprehension of the character of government. They forget to consider that government is the effect rather than the cause of any great good or great evil.

"That government is best, which is best administered."

THE CAUSE OF AFRICAN SLAVERY.

It is not the silent letter of the law which enslaves the African, or restricts a single privilege of his race. He was a slave at home before he was brought to America. He is now a slave. Free him in the slave States, where he is not in a majority of the population, and society would subject him to the same oppressive laws which are now brought to bear him down. That is now true. It is the prejudice and cupidity of the white man, and the ignorance and imbecility of the black man, which indicates the relative condition of each, and fixes the law of their respective power and consequent submission.

What is the condition of the negro in the northern States, where the ratio of blacks to whites is such, that the blacks are scarcely a constituent element of society? Is it not true that prejudice and malice have virtually robbed the negro of every conceivable source of happiness and right? In what northern State is this not true in relation to the free negro as a class? In Indiana, in Illinois, and in Iowa it is a crime, with a degrading penalty, for any negro or mulatto to emigrate to those States. Even in New England—in Puritan New England, the Land of the Pilgrims—the black man need aspire to no higher position than that of a master barber, head cook, or hotel boot-black. This is the outside limit of his social position as a class. An individual exception to the rule there may be. The prejudice is overpowering, and, poor unfortunate man, he is made to feel it wherever he goes. It eats as a canker in his bosom; it burns as a fever in his blood.

In the South the proportion of the blacks to the whites is nearly as two to three. Here they are in slavery. That occasional wrong may be done them by cruel masters, is quite likely. That they have received more than their due proportion of the injuries allotted by Divine Providence to the human race, may also be true; but, under the circumstances that surround them, in both the North and the South, that they suffer in person, in privilege, in character, in social regard, in the latter more than they suffer in the former section of the Union, is not true.

In the South the police regulation places them on the plantation, subjected to plantation rules, among people of their own color, of their own kindred in the place of their birth. Interest, affection, and association bind the master and his family to the slave and his family; and it is a remarkable fact, that when the two families have grown up together, so mutual are the attachments and regard, that slavery ceases in every other except its legal sense. In the North, excluded from society, the jail is the penalty inflicted upon them for the exhibition of those infirmities common to their race, which are scarcely recognised in southern law as crimes in the conduct of the slave, under the rule of heartless prison-keepers, inured to cruelty, and dead to every sentiment of kindness.

Prejudice and false accusations bear him down and contribute to his misfortunes in the northern States; for there he has not even a master to look after his rights and defend him against the encroachments of unscrupulous men who with impunity may rob him of the wages of his labor, outrage his feelings, and ruin his character.

It is unphilosophical, impracticable, and without a single precedent in the history of human government, that any race or any individual can gain social position until he has triumphed over social prejudices. These prejudices are co-extensive with his being. On the American continent they meet him wherever he goes. At the table he is a waiter—never a guest; from the common school his child is excluded a place with the child of the white man. It is true that in the church he communes with God through the sacred emblems of the body and blood of his Saviour, but not until after the white man has partaken of these precious tokens of the love of God. In court he may be a criminal, or he may perform the duties of a menial servant, but he is excluded from the bench, the bar, the jury-box, and even from the witness stand, though it be to protect his own most precious rights. Is this liberty? Yet such is the condition of the black man even in the mighty FREE NORTH.

There is a prejudice which underlies the law, much stronger than the law itself. Until that prejudice is removed the condition of the black man must remain deplorable. He will seek refuge in that condition of society which gives him protection, though it be in the degraded relation of slavery. What has been his treatment in the North? In Philadelphia, mobs have raised to drive him from the city. In Cincinnati he has been hunted down like a wolf. When the slaves of John Randolph left the plantation cottages of old Virginia to seek a home upon that *rich free soil*, so liberally granted by Virginia to the

Union—those unfortunate men who had lingered round the mansion of the Roanoke orator, and never knew that they had been slaves until they were freed, and found slavery in freedom; when, after many weeks' hard travel, old men, women, and children sought a home of freedom upon their own land, they were met by an armed band and driven away and hunted down as outlaws. Added to the prejudices against the black man are the interests of the white laboring classes, who, in competition with him, will destroy his business, or, in failing to effect this, will engage in the extermination of his race.

In answer to these plain practical questions, which admit of no cavil that is beyond all successful contradiction, we are tauntingly asked, is the black man a brute? Certainly not. He is an immortal man, with a soul that will burn in brilliant beauty long after the fires of the sun have died out. Why, then, this state of slavery? For the most humane of all reasons: for the protection of those very rights which are invaded by prejudice; for the expansion and development of those very minds—jewels that have been buried in the darkness of idolatry for ages.

The southern people have been insulted, aroused, and inflamed by libellous publications, until, under the goading of intermeddlers, they have passed some laws which are unnecessary and unnatural, but which lie as a dead letter upon the statute-book, as a record of misguided feeling, which are scarcely ever executed. It is barbarous to tear asunder the bonds of matrimony; it is sacrilegious to lay waste the family altar; but, unfortunately for our unhappy race, we have never been elevated above these misfortunes; they transpire daily in every portion of the earth; under the cover of law they ought never to take place, and the South owe it to the good name of their ancestors to modify those laws, correct these evils; and if left undisturbed by abolitionists, they would do it. In the north, capital is arrayed against labor, and the sweat that falls from the brow of the mechanic and common laborer is only so much capital speculated upon by the capitalist who never labors. This state of things has always existed; it will most likely always continue; all efforts have failed to bring to bear efficient correctives; in the very effort to correct, a greater evil may ensue.

Slavery is only one form of evil growing out of the effort to govern men, and it happens to be located and identified with the South. Have we any evils in the north, or in the general government, which bear unequally upon the different classes of the country? Our great government is rich—rich in mines, in resources, in yearly products; she is affluent, without a peer in the civilized world. She ought to be magnanimous to the poorer classes of her own people; she ought to be just. But what do we see? Does not the laboring man pay a heavy tax upon the salt that seasons his victuals; upon the shirt and pants with which he is clothed; on the calico dress of his wife, and the shoes of his children; upon the iron in his plough; upon his hoe, his gears, and upon the oil which preserves them? It is a heavy tax he pays. While the property of the rich man—his lands, his bank and railroad stocks, his pianos, his library—is taxed only one per cent., the poor man pays nearly forty per cent. upon nearly all the necessaries of life. Such is the justice dealt out to the poor man north and south. But this injustice is aggravated when the applications of the moneys are fairly tabled. Why is this tax levied upon him—upon the poor man, who has not a comfortable cabin in which to live? The first answer is, to give incidental protection to the business of the rich man, who lives in the style of an eastern prince—to the manufacturer of the northern States. After this money is thus raised, how is it spent? Why, to pay for public documents, engraved sea-voyage reports, electioneering campaign books, which are sent to the leaders of party, or to the parlors of the wealthy and fashionable, but never to the poor man's cabin, or the workshop of the laborer. Look at this statement:

The poor laboring man's salary is $20 per month, or per year, of 12 months, $240. His clothing for himself and family costs $100; of this $100, $40 is tariff on his clothes.

Making just one sixth of his whole salary, to say nothing of his taxes upon the necessaries of life. How are the proceeds of this robbery upon labor applied? Why, a very large amount of it is squandered and pilfered; some of it is appropriated to buy books to send to his rich neighbors. Just think of it—one sixth of the ordinary laborer's wages, two months of every year, given to government, every cent of which is absolutely necessary for the decent support of himself and family; more than enough to pay the tuition of his children is filched from him by officials, stolen quietly from him before it has been in his pocket; yes, taken from him to buy books for his landlord, or applied to protect the capital of manufacturing earls. This is unjust, oppressive, outrageous. The wrong is magnified when it is properly considered that the wealth of the country is boundless. Her public lands are a national fund that ought to yield sufficient for the support of government economically administered; but how are they disposed of? For the benefit of the poor? No. Do the poor have equal chances in the sales of them? No. Is it not true that by the general government these lands are given in immense bodies to rich companies to create monopolies, which will ultimately control the country? The injustice of this will be more apparent when more thoroughly presented, so that the government may lose nothing in the creation of these mammoth monopolies. Provision is made to raise the price of the poor man's land just one hundred per cent., and this injustice, which will create invidious classes in the society of the white man, has met with no opposition except from the South.

Many other evils than domestic slavery, contravening the very same principles of human rights which are involved in it, and which are suffered by white men, call loudly for legislative remedy, where we have the unquestionable legislative power to control the evil Why not save all this argument? This party does not so much as propose the abolition of slavery. The men of the Republican party repel the insinuation that they have intimated the emancipation of the negroes. They do not so much as propose to free one human being, not one. It is the *ground* which they propose to emancipate, the soil which they intend to free. They protest that they want none of the black population, either free or slave.

In a late article in answer to the charge that Mr. Fremont is a slaveholder, the Tribune denies that any such issue is made against slaveholders as would exclude them from any high official position and power. The whole is reduced down to the bare question of FREE-SOIL.

FREE SOIL.

The most specious, transparent, captivating, and yet unmeaning word in the whole nomenclature of political claptrap, is this word FREE SOIL. It is one of those apparent synonyms of benevolence which carries to the idle mind a splendid promise, and means less than nothing at all. It addresses itself to the love of liberty, and the rights of man. Yet it really proposes to do no one act which can directly or remotely benefit the negro, as a race, or as a single individual. If freedom to the black man be his natural right, the FREE-SOIL party does not propose to secure it to one single negro or mulatto. If it be a political blessing, this *Free-soil* party has not an offer of it to one single child of the downtrodden race of Ham. It does not offer freedom to anybody; but, on the contrary, the history of this FREE-SOIL movement carries with it a single series of proscriptions to the black man and the white man both. It began by excluding the right of white men to carry slaves within its borders; but soon the real character of this movement was manifest. It was quite apparent that this warfare was not against slavery as a system, but against the Africans as a race, for in Ohio he was long excluded the State by the most savage laws, whilst he voted in North Carolina and Pennsylvania when they were both slave States. In Kentucky and South Carolina, in Tennessee and North Carolina, the negro may be a large property-holder, if free; whilst in Illinois, in Indiana, and in Iowa, it is a crime for a black man to seek a home ON THIS FREE SOIL. Indiana and Illinois were the offspring of the ordinance of 1787; yet by the constitution of Indiana, the blacks are excluded the State, and are thereby declared unfit for freedom, whilst in Illinois a poor wayfaring African may be sold out for venturing to rest his limbs on their *free soil*. Nor did BARBOUR, JOHN U. PETTIT, and MACE, then prominent Democrats, now *Free-soil* leaders of their party in the State of Indiana, see any wrong done to the blacks in this exclusion, for, notwithstanding this proscription, it still remained FREE SOIL. In the State of Indiana a black man may be stricken down, his son may be beaten, his wife and daughter may be violated in his presence by the vilest white men; and without even a master to redress his wrong, or pursue the enemy of his household, the poor African, though half his blood be Anglo Saxon, would not dare even file an information affidavit setting forth his wrongs, or seeking redress for his injuries. Whilst in South Carolina the free black may make affidavit for himself; and the master may, on behalf of his slave. Nor does a white man dare employ the black man in Indiana, under heavy penalties; yet this is *free soil*, made so by the ordinance of 1787.

When TRUMBULL, and BISSELL, and LINCOLN, and the illustrious JOHN WENTWORTH led the van of the Illinois Democracy, those laws were enacted which make it a crime, with the penalty of a forfeiture of liberty, for a black man to breathe the atmosphere or set his feet upon the *free soil* of Illinois. Yet, this is a part of the Territory made *free* by the ordinance of 1787, and these gentlemen are the benevolent leaders of the *Free-soil* party. Iowa was the first-born daughter of the Missouri compromise, and punishes with imprisonment any negro or mulatto who ventures emigration to her *free soil.*

Lord Mansfield says that no slave can breathe the air of Great Britain; so no black man can tread the *free soil* of those "ORDINANCE," and "COMPROMISE," and "SACRED COMPACT" *Free-soil* States. As though to complete the solemn farce and tinsel the grave burlesque of free soil, in the struggle for conquest in Kansas, the framers of the Topeka constitution were careful that free negroes and mulattoes should be excluded the contemplated *free-soil* State.

Government cannot be applied to soil. Government is the ruling law of men—rational men; and there is just as much good sense in talking of free vegetation, and less absurdity in speaking of free horses, than in speaking of free soil. This party does not propose to enlighten the black man and elevate his mental aspirations. It does not propose to educate him, and prepare him for a higher state of social being. It does not propose to give him one cent for his moral culture or his religious improvement. It proposes to make him a pretext for official promotion and public plunder.

Now, honestly, what do they mean by free soil? Throwing off the circumlocutions of language, the flowers of rhetoric, and the new-coined nomenclature of party phraseology, does it not mean, practically, about this: A soil from which all Africans are excluded—a mere Shibboleth of disappointed political aspirants to catch up honest and well-disposed yet deluded men, for the mere sake of personal preferment and political POWER?

THE RELATIVE POSITION OF THE NORTH AND SOUTH TO SLAVERY IN THE UNITED STATES.

That is not a bad law of benevolence which demands that "A man should be just before he is generous;" nor is that an unreasonable law of gentility which indicates that every man should exemplify his precepts by his actions. And upon these two unquestionably just principles do we now examine the superior claims to benevolence of the free States as against the slave States.

To correctly determine their relative position of regard and love for the African race, we subjoin the following table. There were, in the year 1850, in the slave States—

	Free negroes.
Alabama	2,265
Arkansas	608
District of Columbia	10,059
Delaware	18,075
Florida	932
Georgia	2,931
Kentucky	10,011
Louisiana	17,462
Maryland	74,723
Mississippi	930

Missouri	2,618
North Carolina	27,463
South Carolina	8,960
Tennessee	6,422
Texas	397
Virginia	54,333
	238,209

Slaves freed by legislation in what are now free States.

California	
Connecticut	2,759
Illinois	917
Indiana	237
Iowa	16
Maine	2
Massachusetts	1
Michigan	32
New Hampshire	158
New Jersey	7,557
New York	20,343
Ohio	6
Pennsylvania	3,737
Rhode Island	952
Vermont	17
Wisconsin	
	36,734

In making this estimate I allow that the highest number of slaves which were ever held at any one time in those States which are now free were freed by legislation. But we may justly make a deduction of those slaves which were sold, and those which were freed by voluntary emancipation, amounting, together, to at least one-fourth of the whole number of slaves in those States. Then the tables stand thus:

Originally	36,734
Freed and sold—one-fourth	9,183
Leaving	27,551

which were freed by legislation in the free States, whilst (including their descendants) 238,209 negroes have been freed by voluntary emancipation in the slave States.

This calculation excludes those negroes who were emancipated in slave States, and emigrated to the free States. The foregoing table proves, that in the slave States, where there is a population of 9,664,656, there are 238,209 free negroes, or one free negro in forty persons; whilst in the free States, where there is a population of 13,434,922, there is a free negro population of 195,071, or one free negro in every sixty-nine of the population; which is a demonstration of the fact that

the negroes are freed by voluntary emancipation quite as rapidly as they prove themselves capable of enjoying liberty.

Free negroes in the free States.

California	17
Connecticut	7,693
Illinois	5,436
Indiana	11,262
Iowa	333
Maine	1,356
Massachusetts	9,064
Michigan	2,583
New Hampshire	520
New Jersey	23,810
New York	49,069
Pennsylvania	53,626
Ohio	25,279
Rhode Island	3,670
Vermont	718
Wisconsin	635
	195,071

This table shows that even now there are more free negroes in the slave States than in the free States.

The above tables prove that the moral power of the country, by elevating the moral condition of the slave, has done for him infinitely more than all political power and political causes put together. And it may be very properly submitted to the nothern people, whether it is not their duty to contribute as much, in proportion to their wealth and population, to the freedom of the slave as the South has already done, before they open their mouths in reproach against the South.

The foregoing tables demonstrate several things:

1st. That the emancipation of slaves in most of the free States amounted to a merely nominal abolition, for there were very few slaves in those States to free.

2d. That the benevolence and philanthropy of the abolitionists have exhibited more of the spirit of officious intermeddling than any one real desire for the real good of the slave.

In the year 1850, in the slave States there were voluntarily manumitted 1,467 slaves, which is 46 more than were ever freed by legislative enactment in all of the States of VERMONT, MAINE, MASSACHUSETTS, IOWA, WISCONSIN, OHIO, NEW HAMPSHIRE, MICHIGAN, and INDIANA, all of which were once slaveholding States; and in the same year there were nearly as many slaves, fugitives from the slave States, as were thus freed by the above States. These figures can't lie; these facts are undeniable.

So much for the principles involved in the slavery element of this contest.

So far this party is an illustrated national fraud committed upon the country—a most glaring imposition upon a large body of its supporters. This trick has been made complete. The last stroke of policy is the most uncandid of all the rest. It is the attempt, by bullying and denunciation, to drive the northern wing of the Whig party, without protest, into the support of the men and measures of this new organization. The Whig party had no legitimate connexion with this movement. It is an abandonment of all her ancient principles to affiliate with it. Forgetting former contests, abandoning former principles, under the captious lead of mere upstart politicians, who have in form and in act ostracised statesmanship who assume control over the masses, which the masses have not conferred upon them, or invited them to, this party draw black lines around the names of high-minded, honorable men, who refuse to lend their aid to civil war and revolution. *Traitor* and *doughface* are names applied to every northern man who eschews the fanaticism of this party. Where such authority is assumed, and such means are employed to slander the fair character and browbeat into debasing submission the most honorable body of conservative men now in the country, it is a duty we owe to civil liberty and to contemporaneous history to expose these pretensions—to rebuke these assumptions.

By what right do these men call any Whig to account for not adhering to *their* party? The two parties have not one element of character in common.

1. The Whig party, as pledged by its platforms, was conservative, peace-making, law-abiding: the Republican party is ultra, aggressive, and revolutionary.

2. The Whig party was a great *constructive* political organization, that gave to the country its first impulses to internal improvement and domestic manufactures. It proposed the development of our great national resources, the building of railroads, the fortification of the seaboard, and the improvement of her harbors. In the contemplation of the great Whig party, the productive power of every valley, the grass upon every hill, the mineral in the bosom of the mountain, and the crystal streams that washed by the mountain side, were so many varied investments by the God of nature for the improvement, and blessing, and comfort of the citizen, and the glory of the country.

On the other hand, the Republican party is a *destructive* organization, that proposes to invade the present state of society with radical changes; that counsels the resistance to law with the force of arms and the violence of civil war, and threatens, if its dictates are not complied with, to destroy the nation itself.

That immortal Whig, Daniel Webster, said: "Liberty and union, now and forever, one and inseparable." Republican Banks says: "Let the Union slide."

3. The Whig party was comprehensive, liberal, and patriotic. The Republican party have narrowed down the issues of a campaign and the destinies of the republic to one idea, and that idea is one which has no legitimate connexion with politics. They have proscribed every man as a "*doughface*," a "*traitor*," a "*sycophant*," who does not take the same view of questions of public policy which they do. They de-

clare contempt for even the preservation of the country, if it be not preserved by their own party, and upon their own terms.

4. The Whig party did not shrink from contest, though she never invited it. She met it when it was offered her; but it was the conflict of mind with mind in the discussion of great principles, in the determination of great truths. The speeches of Clay, Webster, Clayton, Berrien, Preston, Crittenden, Rives, and Bell, will go down to posterity as congressional history, and their memories will be held in precious remembrance as long as true oratory has an admirer, or civil liberty a friend.

The Republican party invites contest and provokes quarrel; but it is the contest of passion and prejudice—the virus of envy infused from the poisoned tongue of slander and thrown into the life-blood of the body politic; the contest of jealousy, whose infernal fires are fanned by detraction and fed by falsehood; the contest of malignity that hunts down the living, that throws its missiles at the good name of the absent, and, jackall-like, howls around the sepulchres of the illustrious dead. Nor is it the quarrel of contending parties, aroused by a sense of injustice done them and fearless of conflict and death. It is the bandying of epithets, the inauguration into the council chambers of the country of the vernacular of the billiard saloon and the billingsgate of the beershop.

5. The Whig platform embraced not one single article or principle contained in the late Republican manifesto of doctrines.

6. The great *leaders* of the old Whig party have declined participation in the movement of the Republican party, whilst most of the prominent of that party have sought other political affinities. Among the men who, in the palmy days of Whig honor, and power, and glory, enjoyed its confidence and led its forces, were Rufus Choate, Robert C. Winthrop, and Edward Everett, of Massachusetts; John M. Clayton, of Delaware; William C. Rives, George W. Summers, A. H. H. Stewart, of Virginia; W. C. Preston, Waddy Thompson, of South Carolina; Robert Toombs, A. H. Stevens, Crawford, and Jenkins, of Georgia; H. W. Hilliard, of Alabama; Benjamin, of Lousiana; John Bell, James C. Jones, Neil Brown, of Tennessee; John J. Crittenden, the Marshalls and Breckinridges, and John B. Thompson, of Kentucky; George E. Badger, Willie P. Mangum, and E. Stanley, of North Carolina; J. A. Pearce, Thomas Pratt, Reverdy Johnson, of Maryland; Richard W. Thompson, of Indiana; Ewing and Corwin, of Ohio; George Evans, of Maine. In view of these facts, what claim has the Republican organization to any consideration whatever from the old Whig party? We have carefully examined every element in the composition of the Republican party. In its nakedness look at its issues. Carefully and thoroughly canvass its claims. On the other hand, the principles of the Whig party are set forth with clearness and directness, without equivocation. Look at them. Is there anything in common in the two parties? But, on the other hand, who leads this Republican party? The great standard-bearer himself is a seceding Democrat by profession. In Massachusetts, Charles Sumner, Henry Wilson, N. P. Banks, who were all originally the political enemies of Daniel

Webster, are now the expounders of the Republican faith. In New York, Preston King; in New Hampshire, John P. Hale; in Maine, Hannibal Hamlin; in Pennsylvania, David Wilmot and G. A. Grow; in Ohio, Leiter and Chase; in Indiana, Barbour, Mace, and John U. Pettit; in Illinois, Lyman Trumbull, John Wentworth, and W. H. Bissell, are the prominent Free-soil leaders. Horace Greeley said that the Whig party is dead, and these seceding Democrats claim the right, without invitation, voluntarily to administer upon the estate and appropriate to themselves the effects, and kindly to act guardian to her orphan children.

Surely no Whig will see political obligations resting upon him to support this new party. Yet, upon their part, no effort will be spared to bully him into submission to, or slander him into acquiescence in their measures as administered by these men.

THE MEANS EMPLOYED TO SECURE SUCCESS.

The composition of this party, the object of its being, the bold issues presented, are not more startling and extraordinary than the means employed for the accomplishment of their purposes.

THE COURSE OF THE OLD ABOLITION PARTY.

The old Abolition party, for the time being, gave way grounds which she had hitherto regarded as essentially sacred; she now slumbered and fell back into the foreground of Republicanism, as it now is.

SECRET LODGES.

In the mean time, in every ward in the cities, in every country village, at every cross-road school-house in the rural districts of the North, lodges were formed, and men bound by oath to support the members of their order in preference to all other persons whatsoever. They used significant pass-words. They made it a point to receive no old politician into their lodges; if he were an honest man, this would have been fatal to their purpose—it would have secured their earlier exposition. They made every manner of pretension, and every variety of purpose was ostensibly set forth in plea for the organization.

To old men, they would argue the necessity of a purification of the government, and, in the degeneracy of the times, they would bring back things to the simplicity and economy of Jefferson, Washington, and Madison.

To the conservative men they presented a gloomy picture of the dangers of the dissolution of the Union, and promised, in this new organization, a great national salvator.

To the office-seekers, who had been disgusted with disappointment, they depicted and deplored the monopolization of the offices of the country by men of foreign birth, and gave, as the basis of the party organization, the ostracism of all foreigners indiscriminately.

To the Protestant, they appealed to the prejudices and passions aroused by ancient religious wars and sectarian persecutions, and gave him assurances that the Catholic interest in the civil government of America should be ignored forever; that no Catholic, nor one whose wife was a Catholic, or who was the supporter of a Catholic, or one who did not join this order to oppose the Catholic in this peculiar manner, should hold any office whatever under the government.

To the *abolitionist* they presented the real issue, and made the true appeal, and promised to seduce thousands from old party affinities, and chain them with oaths, and then direct their votes for the accomplishment of the great free-soil reform.

To young men they promised promotion, and position, and honor, as inducement to commence an early political career.

Political chicanery was reduced to a science, and falsehood formed the basis of the whole organization—conceived in deception, and consummated in a great fraud upon public credulity.

THE PRESS.—SLANDER.

The press is prostituted to corrupt the public mind—inductive reasoning is sneered at; disgraceful epithets manufactured; slanders, the misrepresentation of private business, the vilest assaults upon personal character and domestic life, are the ordinary means employed to excite the public mind. The ruling power is denounced as imbecile and despotic; conservative men are branded with cowardice; the living are attacked in their homes; the unwithering laurels of the illustrious dead are not too precious to be trampled under their feet, nor the sepulchre too sacred to preserve it from the vandal fury of these despoilers.

Burns well said: "That man was scarce o' news, who tauld his father was hanged." And that will be a gloomy day in the history of American literature, when the aspersions made against revolutionary heroes can find *a permanent place in an American library*. By this new party, schools, colleges, universities, are appropriated to the discussion of these topics, and the minds of the young are poisoned with sectional bitterness.

The pulpit, the great conservator of the peace and happiness of the world, is perverted to most extraordinary purposes in this campaign. During the times of the Revolution, churches were used as citadels of defence against the invasion of a foreign enemy who was burning our cities and cornfields, gibbeting our soldiers, and committing indiscriminate slaughter upon men, women, and children. It was right to defend ourselves. The very source of the law-making power was arrayed in war against us. There was no other remedy left for us; it was our duty to fight. In terrible times the temple of God has very appropriately become our city of refuge, and as such has been sacredly regarded even by invaders in every civilized country. But with the law ruling over us—with not one wrong which the law will not speedily redress when applied to—to use the house of God for the purpose of inflaming the passions of the people, to raise in arms to butcher their neighbors, is a high crime against the Prince of Peace, which can admit of no justification whatever, consistent with that "peace on earth, good will to man, glory to God in the highest," which was first sung by the angels at the birth of the Saviour.

But this has been done in New England. Good men have been shocked by these demonstrations; bad men have been licensed by them to go forth and commit crimes and riot; children have watched the movement, and the example will long live in their minds after the precepts of the gospel have been forgotten, and terrible will be the accountability of these men at the bar of Heaven. Weak men have been placed in power by surprise to the people, to the lasting injury of civil government, to the burning shame and disgrace of the country; tricksters, who before had but their chances to run, were by that process secured in their aspirations by oaths exacted from their supporters. Legislative experience has been presented as an objection to official position, and sneered at as a qualification for the performance of official duties. It has become the boast of party men, that *old office-holders* have been displaced, and the representative government is now in the hands of men *fresh* from the people.

With this new party temperance has been ostensibly, but never has been really an issue. Benevolence to the slave has been paraded in the Free-soil platform as the *ultima thule* of the organization; but practically and really the issues are made regardless of his condition or happiness. It is *free soil* they are contending for—*the emancipation of the land* that they insist upon. But they have a real issue with the democratic party, a real object in view, and under a quiet transparent cover of the names of *liberty*, and *morality*, and *temperance*, and *progress*, they are drifting the wind in the distance, and, with keen scent, are following the spoils of office. Many of them complain of their disappointment, and charge home upon the present administration a want of faith in the failure to appreciate their real worth and to reward their real service in the labor of their party. This class of gentlemen have been trimming for a life-time between parties, and, alternately fed and famishing between party spoils and party disappointment, they are most furious in their warfare. Disappointed at every stage of their political life, they are quite profuse in their political vituperation; "ten thousand thousands are their throats, but only teats for one." It is a misfortune in this government that the executive office is encumbered by an oppressive patronage such as now encumbers it.

In the incoming of each administration, instead of this class of men, expecting, as they should, that the powers of the government will be directed to the ends of justice, they would have, and try to make scenes, at and after the inauguration of President of the United States, with their scrambles for office, like the western land sales, where bids and clubs are alternately used to buy, and intimidate buyers. Finding no one so corrupt as themselves, they go away dissatisfied; and failing to make honorable men subserve their purposes, they commence a warfare upon those in office, without respect to either their character or qualifications.

OFFICE, POWER, and PATRONAGE, are the real issues with these men; and to gain them, they dare present other issues as contingencies, upon the failure of which, in this party contest, civil war is offered as the alternative of defeat with them.

The issue now made up is not equivocal, but clear, well defined, and terrible. Read it from the New York Tribune, and the leading papers of that party:

"We urge, therefore, unbending determination on the part of the northern members hostile to this intolerable outrage, and demand of them, in behalf of peace—in behalf of freedom—in behalf of justice and humanity—resistance to the last. Better that confusion should ensue—better that discord should reign in the national councils—*better that Congress should break up in wild disorder—nay, better that the Capitol itself should blaze by the torch of the incendiary*, or fall and bury all its inmates beneath its crumbling ruins, than that this perfidy and wrong should be finally accomplished."

This invites results which the noblest impulses of human hope can scarcely outlive. It is couched in language as violent, reckless, revolutionary, and incendiary, as words and sentences can make it.

To the citizens of the whole country these issues are addressed in tens of thousands of copies of that vindictive sheet scattered over the land. The question is not *liberty* or *slavery*, Whig or Democrat, or even Free-soil and Democracy, giving to each their legitimate chances among an honorable and liberty-loving people; but it is, shall Republicanism triumph, and the country perish in the struggle? and whether it is of no matter "*that the Capitol itself should blaze by the torch of the incendiary.*" This is, then, the unmistakable issue drawn out by their leaders before the country. "Rule or ruin" is their motto. Their object in the coming campaign is the spoils of office, or the dissolution of the Union.

The following paragraphs cannot be easily misapprehended—read them:

REPUBLICANISM AND DISUNION.

JOHN P. HALE,

The abolition candidate for President against Scott and Pierce in 1852: What is his record? On the 7th of February, 1850, he presented, insisted upon, and along with Chase and Seward alone, voted to receive, refer, and consider a petition demanding of Congress "an immediate dissolution of the Union," because a union with slaveholders is violative of divine law and human rights. Cass, Corwin, Benton, Clay, and Webster, with forty-six other Senators, voted against it.

On the 23d of March, 1848, he presented a batch of eight petitions at once demanding the same thing.

BENJAMIN F. WADE.

Hear him:

"He thought there was but one issue before the people, and that was the question of American slavery. He said the whig party is not only dead but stinks. It shows signs occasionally of convulsive spasms, as is sometimes exhibited in the dead snake's tail, after the head and body have been buried.

"There is really no union now between the North and the South, and he believed no two nations upon the earth entertained feelings of more bitter rancor towards each other than these two nations of the republic."

N. P. BANKS, JR.,

The "Union slider" Speaker of the abolition House of Representatives, is a leader of the Fremont party, and was withdrawn from the candidacy of the Know-nothing seceders' convention to make way for Fremont. Hear him:

"Although I am not one of that class of men who cry for the perpetuation of the Union, though I am willing in a certain state of circumstances to let it slide, I have no fear for its perpetuation. But let me say, if the chief object of the people of this country be to maintain and propagate chattel property in man—in other words, human slavery—this Union cannot and ought not to stand."

HORACE MANN.

Hear him:

"In conclusion, I have only to add that such is my solemn and abiding conviction of the character of slavery, that, under a full sense of my responsibilty to my country and my God, I deliberately say, better disunion—better a civil or a servile war—better anything that God in his Providence shall send—than an extension of the bonds of slavery."

CHARLES SUMNER.

Hear him:

"The good citizen as he reads the requirements of this act—the fugitive slave—is filled with horror. * * Here the path of duty is clear I AM BOUND TO DISOBEY THIS ACT."

"Sir, I will not dishonor this home of the Pilgrims and of the Revolution by admitting—nay, I cannot believe—that this bill will be executed here."

RUFUS P. SPALDING

Was a member and leader of the convention. Hear him:

"In the case of the alternative being presented of the continuance of slavery or a dissolution of the Union, I am for dissolution of the Union. I am for dissolution, and I care not how quick it comes."

HON. ERASTUS HOPKINS,

Of Massachusetts, was a member of the convention. Hear him:

"If peaceful means fail us, and we are driven to the last extremity where ballots are useless then we'll make bullets effective." [Tremendous applause.]

GEN. JAMES WATSON WEBB

Was a leader in the convention. Hear him in a speech on the floor:

"On the action of this convention depends the fate of the country; if the 'Republicans' fail at the ballot-box, we will be forced to drive back the slaveocracy with fire and the sword." [Cheers.]

Hear also H. M. ADDISON, of the American Advertiser, in the same strain:

"I detest slavery, and say unhesitatingly that I am in favor of its abolition by some means, if it should send all the party organizations in the Union, and *the Union itself, to the devil!* If it can only exist by holding millions of human beings in the most abject and cruel system of slavery that ever cursed the earth, it is *a great pity it was ever formed, and the sooner it is dissolved the better.*"

ANSON BURLINGAME

A Massachusetts member of Congress, is also a leader of the Fremont party. Hear him:

"The times demand, and we must have, an anti-slavery constitution, an anti-slavery Bible, and an anti-slavery God."

CIVIL WAR AND DISSOLUTION.

This issue they do not prosecute in bold, open, manly warfare. They propose to weaken and undermine, and then overthrow the government. They set up imaginary standards of right, to which all laws must conform, and to which all legislation must be subservient. If laws are *unjust*, *cruel*, or *wrong*, according to their standard, they do not propose their repeal by the law-making power, but counsel armed resistance to law. If laws are unconstitutional, they do not propose their abrogation by an appeal to the judiciary—the constitutional remedy for the correction of unconstitutional laws; but that the *constitution*, *law*, and *government* itself shall fall a prey to the maddened mob—a victim to the fury of the licentious multitude. Is not the spectacle now presented to the country alarming and terrible? *Martial* law exists in Washington Territory; Indian war in Oregon. There is revolution in California and civil war in Kansas, and a licentiousness in Utah that burlesques all Christian government.

These demonstrations of lawlessness are not mere spontaneous outbursts of passion in different portions of the country; they are the legitimate fruits of the teachings of revolutionary men who seek refuge from imaginary wrongs in lawless anarchy.

In Boston, in the name of God and religion, officers of the law were shot down by an irresponsible mob, because they believed the fugitive-slave law unconstitutional. The Supreme Court of the United States could have been very properly appealed to to determine this great legal question.

But as though to make the triumph of mob-law *supreme*, the judgment of the Supreme Court is challenged in the United States Senate as time-serving, and the court itself is characterized as the citadel of slavery.

In Wisconsin the leading citizens join in a mob to liberate a slave. The highest State judicial tribunal defends the lawless course by deciding a question over which it had no jurisdiction whatever.

But when to mobs is surrendered the rule of the country, like other bodies invested with discretionary power, they are by no means so ready to surrender it as they were to receive it. They deem the "fugitive-slave law" unconstitutional, and oppose its execution. But these same gentlemen take it into their heads that imprisonment for life, though it be the extent of the law, is not a sufficient punishment for the crime of murder, nor the sheriff the proper officer to enforce law. They follow the indications of high judicial decisions. In another case they arrest the prisoner from the hands of the law, and barbarously drag him to the gallows. This might, by a bare possibility, be doing no injustice in an individual instance, but it does violence to that legal security without which there cannot long exist either justice or law. These outbreaks are spreading over the land. They are spreading under the auspices of a perverted judiciary. They are supported by ministers of religion who have subsidized the temple of God, and prostituted the Sabbath of Christian civilization for the raising of fire-arms, the commission of murder, and the plotting of treason against the liberties of the people and the perpetuity of the government under the sanctity of the hallowed name of duty and brotherly love.

Lawless men will take courage from, and plead the precedent of these nullifiers of law and justice and order. If this party is sustained by the popular vote, it may yet come upon us at a day near at hand, that other cities than San Francisco may establish martial law, and send forth guerrilla bands to the rural districts to *regulate* the affairs of the country; for if it be right to violate law in Boston to free a slave, it will be right to take him by force from Missouri or Maryland; and for all this they will plead precedent—precedent established by the staid people of Boston, precedent set by Puritan divines, precedent made and approved under the auspices and patronage of a *liberty*-loving people, precedent sustained by the judiciary of Wisconsin.

With this state of things, soon will follow the entire rupture of communications between the States, and then the destruction of commerce. And our navy and merchantmen, following the example of judges and divines, will, in the wild spirit of free-booting and plunder, engage in war to free the slaves along the sea-board, and baptise the ocean with the blood of their countrymen; this will soon induce a general border war all along the line. Intercepting marauding companies will engage in tearing up railroads that have cost years of labor and millions of money. Parties made up of street loafers, prison convicts, headed by adventurous men without principle, without property, and without stake in the country, will sally forth on each side of the black and bloody line of the contending sections to lay waste farms, and light up the dwellings of innocent men with the bonfires of midnight. Our great nation, which fed starving Ireland only yesterday, on to-morrow will, unless these flagrant outrages cease, engage in cutting the throats of poor distracted Americans.

By fanning this flame—by a dissolution of the Union, such as is proposed in the extracts above. the misguided politicians of New England will throw out of employment her millions of citizens. The shop, the loom, and the anvil will cease their murmuring music, and tens of thousands of the restless men who are now waging war against the peace of the country will be found clamoring for bread, and driving from their bosom the factious leaders who have sown this spirit of national discord among them—who have blighted their highest hopes and thwarted their holiest aspirations. In this anarchy, the necessary result of these doctrines, bands of regulators will be instituted to correct the evils and promote the good of the country; trial by jury, the determination of legal questions by the ordinary process of regular government, will be entirely too slow and uncertain for these reformers.

Then will the press gather its freedom from the dictum of alternate factions, which will in turn assume to rule the various fragments of our mutilated country. Free speech will be under the same iron rule, regulated by like passions of like men. Then will Republican, American, Fourrierite, Abolitionist, each in their turn play Jack Ketch, or perish on the gibbet, just as fortune or power may smile or frown upon them. Nor will the writ of *habeas corpus*—the birthright of every American, the last hope of injured innocence—avail anything. With the revolutionary remnants of our ruptured government, Dante, Marat, and Robespierre, peers of Nero, Commodus, and Caligula—names that have marked the ultra limits of incarnated despotism, cruelty, and crime—will be pleaded in precedent for the justification of all these outrages, and necessity will be the broad principle upon which apology will be offered in defence of these infernal wrongs; these crimes against civilization and Christianity—against earth and Heaven.

Nor will the rights of conscience be any better preserved than the liberty of speech. Another inquisitorial age may succeed, when the opinions of men may be tortured from them, and traps be laid to entrammel them, and star-chambers may be instituted, and their own frank testimony turned against honest men to secure their conviction and insure their destruction. In this heated fanaticism these men will fancy themselves religious, and in the holy name of Christianity they will doom Christians to expiate their heresy at the stake or on the scaffold.

Nor will these things stop here. Temples of God will be lighted up by the torch of the bigot and incendiary, just as contending parties are victorious or defeated—each crimination and recrimination, each suffering and consequent revenge, assuming a more terrible character and attended by a more horrible tragedy. Nor will our more enlightened character render these conflicts less disastrous. This very fact will call into requisition a greater power to perpetrate a more furious outrage and consummate a more grievous wrong. In this wreck nothing will be preserved.

Our character, too, will then go, in this general destruction of country. Surely our good name is precious to the heart of every American. America has been the home of the oppressed of every nation and kindred and tongue. Her name has been a sure guaranty of human rights to her citizens in foreign lands. The American name is now a passport of honor among every people under the whole heavens. The American republic yet stands as an exception—in the vigor of her youth and in the strength of her manhood—to the doctrine that republics cannot endure. Her magnanimity in war, her benevolence in peace, her kindness to her own people, and her hospitality to strangers, gives her a character everywhere. And must this, too, fall a sacrifice to the mad ambition of reckless men? Is there nothing too sacred for the invasion of this exterminating legion of government reformers?

Her fame must go with it.—In such a destiny, the story of her battle-fields must pass down to posterity as the legends of the skirmishes of restless rebels, who madly dreamed of the permanent establishment of liberal institutions and republican government, and to control and preserve them enacted the farce of self-government. Let this Union be dissolved, and the story of the battles of Bunker Hill and King's Mountain will not be put in either contrast or comparison by our ruined offspring; then the precious memories of those immortal heroes who surrendered their lives to their country and their spirits to God, as a voluntary offering for freedom, will be obliviated, to open up the pathway of glory to despots and usurpers, who would desecrate the temple of liberty, and sacrifice its inmates; who would pollute the altars of Heaven with the blood of their kindred, and, in the insulted name of Christian liberty, would doom their posterity to a hundred ages of hopeless despotism.

The issue is theirs; made up in their own words. It is not deductvie merely; it is not an inference; it is not painted. Look at it—read it. It is this:

Pure Christianity *vs.* Fourrierism, Socialism, and New England Atheism Practical Government *vs.* Visionary Society. The Perpetuity, Prosperity, and Glory of the American Union *vs.* The Wild Forays of Sectional Adventurers and Impracticable Fanaticism.

The determination of this whole question will depend, in a great measure, upon the action of that honorable body of men who stood by the destinies of the country under the lead of Henry Clay, and who will eschew sectionalism, and never cease to honor the proud name and cherish the noble character of

NATIONAL WHIG.

www.ingramcontent.com/pod-product-compliance
Lightning Source LLC
LaVergne TN
LVHW011134110826
845150LV00008B/2333

* 9 7 8 1 4 1 8 1 9 4 0 3 1 *